Pebble® Plus

Looking at Animal Parts

Let's Look at Animal Noses

by Wendy Perkins

Consulting Editor: Gail Saunders-Smith, PhD

Consultant: Suzanne B. McLaren, Collections Manager
Section of Mammals, Carnegie Museum of Natural History
Edward O'Neil Research Center, Pittsburgh, Pennsylvania

Capstone
press®

Mankato, Minnesota

Pebble Plus is published by Capstone Press,
151 Good Counsel Drive, P.O. Box 669, Mankato, Minnesota 56002.
www.capstonepress.com

1 2 3 4 5 6 11 10 09 08 07 06

Library of Congress Cataloging-in-Publication Data
Perkins, Wendy, 1957–
    Let's look at animal noses / by Wendy Perkins.
    p. cm.—(Pebble plus. Looking at animal parts)
    Summary: "Simple text and photographs present animal noses, how they work, and how different animals
use them"—Provided by publisher.
    Includes bibliographical references and index.
    ISBN-13: 978-0-7368-6351-3 (hardcover)
    ISBN-10: 0-7368-6351-6 (hardcover)
    1. Nose—Juvenile literature. I. Title. II. Series.
QL947.P47 2007
599.14′4—dc22   2006001000

Editorial Credits
Sarah L. Schuette, editor; Kia Adams, set designer; Renée Doyle, cover production; Kelly Garvin, photo
    researcher/photo editor

Photo Credits
Image Source/elektraVision, cover
Minden Pictures/Frans Lanting, 12–13; Heidi & Hans-Jurgen Koch, 18–19; Thomas Mangelsen, 9
Nature Picture Library/Aflo, 11; Tony Heald, 16–17
Robert McCaw, 6–7
Seapics/David B. Fleetham, 14–15
Shutterstock/Karlos A. Pedraza, 4–5; Wendy Kaveney Photography, 1; Zachary Garber, 21

Note to Parents and Teachers

The Looking at Animal Parts set supports national science standards related to
life science. This book describes and illustrates animal noses. The images support
early readers in understanding the text. The repetition of words and phrases helps early
readers learn new words. This book also introduces early readers to subject-specific
vocabulary words, which are defined in the Glossary section. Early readers may need
assistance to read some words and to use the Table of Contents, Glossary, Read More,
Internet Sites, and Index sections of the book.

Table of Contents

Noses at Work

Animals breathe
and smell with their noses.
Scents tell animals what's
going on around them.

Sniff, sniff.

A fox smells a rabbit.

The fox sneaks closer.

The rabbit's nose wiggles.

It smells the fox.

Then it hops away to safety.

Kinds of Noses

Horses take in a lot of air
with their large nostrils.
The extra air helps them run
faster and farther.

Hippos stick their wide noses
above water.
They take a big breath
before sinking back under.

Sharks smell food underwater
with their noses.
Sharks have noses
on their snouts.

Elephants lift their long trunks
high in the air.
They smell where to find
water holes.

Pigs sniff the ground
to find food.
Then they use their noses
to dig for the food.

Awesome Animal Noses

Big or small, long or short,
noses help animals breathe
and smell.

Glossary

breathe—to take air in and out of the lungs; many animals use their noses to breathe.

nostril—one of the two openings in a nose through which an animal breathes and smells

scent—an odor

sneak—to move quietly and in secret

snout—the long front part of an animal's head; the nose, mouth, and jaws make up a snout.

trunk—the long nose of an elephant

wiggle—to make small movements from side to side or up and down

Read More

Hall, Peg. *Whose Nose Is This?: A Look At Beaks, Snouts, and Trunks*. Whose Is It? Minneapolis: Picture Window Books, 2003.

Miles, Elizabeth. *Noses*. Animal Parts. Chicago: Heinemann Library, 2003.

Warrick, Karen Clemens. *Who Needs That Nose?* Chanhassen, Minn.: NorthWord Press, 2004.

Internet Sites

FactHound offers a safe, fun way to find Internet sites related to this book. All of the sites on FactHound have been researched by our staff.

Here's how:

1. Visit *www.facthound.com*

2. Choose your grade level.

3. Type in this book ID **0736863516** for age-appropriate sites. You may also browse subjects by clicking on letters, or by clicking on pictures and words.

4. Click on the **Fetch It** button.

FactHound will fetch the best sites for you!

23

Index

Word Count: 134
Grade: 1
Early-Intervention Level: 14